Fleeting, Sacred

Poems by Crista Siglin

Kansas City   Spartan Press   Missouri

Spartan Press
Kansas City, Missouri
spartanpresskc.com

Copyright © Crista Siglin, 2020
Second Edition
ISBN: 978-1-950380-45-9
LCCN: 2019943702

Design, edits and layout: Jeanette Powers,
Jason Ryberg, Iris Appelquist
Cover photos and interior images: Crista Siglin
All rights reserved. No part of this publication may be reproduced or transmitted in any form or by any means, electronic or mechanical, including photocopying, recording or by info retrieval system, without prior written permission from the author.

This book was originally published in May of 2015 as part of the Prospero's POP Poetry series, which ran from 2015 through 2017.

Special thanks to Prospero's Books, Will Leathem, Tom Wayne, Iris Appelquist, M. Scott Douglass and Main Street Rag.

TABLE OF CONTENTS

Once On Land / 1

Water Spiders / 2

The Problem With Invention / 5

Skippy / 7

Should There Ever Be A Door Mat Big Enough / 8

After The Picture Books / 10

Supplant / 12

First Novel / 14

The Shade Of A Truant / 16

Revolutions Around A Mad Woman / 21

Gathering Seeds / 27

An Acquintance / 30

As We View A Union Of Sacred Monsters / 32

In The Time After / 34

Ceramics On The Face / 35

What Needs To Be An Essay / 37

Names / 39

Sharp Pressure / 41

All Legs / 47

Materials For Birth / 48

Outside, The Inside / 50

Fleeting, Sacred

Once, on Land

There is a woman on the sand
(in the sand)

She is turning her hands to driftwood.
She climbs on to a pier.
No,
it's a dining room.
No,
it's a chess board.

There are tiny bipolar men
crawling all over it.

She flicks them
off and they twirl.

There is no gravity in this place.
She sing-songs to them
(once they do not reach the floor)
You are my dear little ghosts.

Water Spiders

We've been caught charting the amount of time
we spend making charts.

We followed thinkers
around the circumference of their time pie.

We were trying to always be at Mount Pisgah,
with dousing rods, walking, waiting for them to cross.

We might have found the tracks of the pioneers, frozen,
thawed, and refrozen.
But maybe we just found the bed where the glaciers once
sat.

We are trying to figure out if we can get all of our sleep
done in one go.

The glaciers melted,
we don't want to melt like they did.

But we do want to think like they did.
We wait before going back to the steps
that we pioneered.

We go back with all our naked, see them, then leave,
go backand are sure to be
equipped with metal, loosely held in our hands
so that we feel the thin L-shaped rods
slowly rotate in our palms when they cross
the spot we crossed.

We only can get to it that way,
sweaty-palmed diviners
ancient and eight years old.

When the snow is deep and the wind is persistent.
it blows into tunnels just tall enough that
we can stand inside them,
we still don't.

We learned in the summer
to watch the water spider's bodies spread out evenly on a
dead pond surface, with disappearing tracks.

We don't want to fall through to the ground,
so we stay on our hands and knees.

The Problem with Invention

An old couple sits near the booth
we sit in
at the Chinese restaurant.
I think
there are two kinds of people.

There are those people
sitting near us in the Chinese restaurant
who keep their menus
after they order so that they can decide
what to eat next time
as they eat what they eat this time.

Then there are those people that
we became as we left the restaurant,
who cut corners
to sit at that part of the intersection
we know has a light
that stays red longer at the point
where we stall.

Every time I stand
I smell sex and two weeks
of cigarettes, coffee, and sweat.
It doesn't bother me
until I'm around my mother.
But then again,
it doesn't seem to bother my father,
so maybe it doesn't bother me.

The man who invented the X-acto knife
also invented a daughter
who's tongue was sharper.
She sliced right through the paper,
through the poem,
and got close enough
to your genitals
to make you scared.

Skippy,

the haunted mansion tour guide
working in Savannah, Georgia.

He calls himself Skippy
because it is approachable.

Skippy tells ghost stories
mostly with fine endings, but the ones
that he takes a drink
of whiskey and coke
afterward, you know
are always still bad
for him in the middle of the night.

One was of a daughter who

Skippy was scared of the same things I was.
The spookiest costumes—
always homemade.

I only had a problem with floating,
scary images when I couldn't get them out.

Should There Ever Be a Doormat Large Enough

To make a monument, you should kill a small bird first.
Then build the foundation of the monument
with its small bones and its small nest.
Spend the rest of your life working to make the monument
much larger than its foundation.

To build a fire, you should always have something breakable
on your person. If it is a worry stone,
put it in your mouth for a while to soften it.
Then throw it on the ground
hard enough to make a crack fumble across its smoothness.
Pick it back up and break it in half.
Use this to spark the first flame after it has dried.

To dull voices in a cathedral, you should fill up two armoires
with cement and
place them where the projection of light
from the stained glass cannot reach them. This way
they will seem pale and sickly,
so visitors will keep their distance.

They should seem like they are ignoring each other,
with the stone grey blouses that
have been coated with the cold
facing people who walk through the echoing space.
Their wooden exteriors should almost scrape each others
backs.

To leave the house, make sure the first steps you take are on
something soft.
If there is not any cloth thick enough to make your feet
only make a thud, pour some water on the porch, and place
your jacket on top of it.

To forget someone, you should place a photograph of their
face in a black frame
surrounded by light bulbs, like the makeup mirror
your mother gave you once.
The wires to the bulbs should be thick, and
incapable of being hidden.

After the Picture Books

I think about the images that are not mine, and the things
I cannot pretend to say.
The image of snow falling does not belong to me.
The image of an old woman
feeding breadcrumbs to the birds
outside the cafe does not belong to me.
A man running toward the image
of a woman standing
at the end of the pier does not belong to me.
The image of a window
on a coffin where the eyes of the body would be belongs to
someone else—although
this window might suggest that no one felt he needed pennies
on his eyelids
to take the ferry that belongs to no one.
The image of me saying, *I am a woman*,
belongs to someone else.

It could be that now I can say these things, because
I have already said them
aloud, but it could be that I cannot make the distinction.

The light bulbs in the lamps of my living room are dim enough so that I cannot see any door frames.
I will tell you fiction is a thing that has never been said aloud, and hope you believe me.
This way I can lie to you without having told a lie.

Supplant

We had caught crawdads one afternoon,
because my sister was not fortunate
when her teacher had drawn names.
My father took us to shallow water.

The water was murky
and impervious. Our reflections
were much more crisp
than the stones at the bottom
of the creek bed.

I once saw
a figure in a window, gazing
at the pane
trying to see their reflection,
rather than the leaves of the tree
barely touching the glass outside.

My mother told me when I lived alone
I should remember
that at night people can see you
through the window from the street,
but you cannot see them.
After the phone conversation
with my step-mother
in the ally behind the bar,
I reminded myself of crawdads,
which had not lived long in our plastic tubs.

We had kept their dried bodies
on a porcelain sink in the basement.
My father threw them in the garden
when he remarried.

First Novel

As you told me that your favorite song was actually about an earthquake,
rather than a girl,
I was trying to make patterns from the numbers
at the top of each square
in the Spanish bingo cards on your wall.

You asked me what I was thinking,
and I mentioned the first book I can remember finishing.

I told you about the part about a lozenge factory
that had shut down.
A woman kept a large quantity of the candies
because they were made to taste sweet and sad.

I didn't think that a candy could taste melancholy;
that they probably only tasted that way
because every time someone ate one,
there would be one less in the world.

When I woke up for the third last time in your bed,
I tried not to let the wooden floor boards announce
my steps to the door.
I gripped the glass doorknob firmly as I turned it to go.

In the afternoon, I twirled a flower
in my fingers, and a boy told me
plants send out chemical distress signals
when part of them is removed.

I thought of summer afternoons when
the wild flower bouquets
in my father's kitchen began to drop petals on the table.
He told my sisters and I that it was bad luck
to keep wilting flowers in the house.

The Shade of a Truant

By the time morning came, and we decided
to go inside, I could see
my fingers were lavender.
Faded lavender was woven
into my uncle's shirts.
In their lavender, angry words
overlap each other.
Again and again
it rains lavender.
Only when the puddles form,
does lavender turn black.
A doll, when it is broken, is lavender.
When the pieces no longer fit together, and the
plastic can't be peach and can't be skin,
it becomes lavender.
Lavender was the color of your eyes
after you leapt
from my moving car.

They were soft after the impact, but
still wanting to crawl back inside me.
Lavender ate my breakfast for me, and
shoved its fist down my throat.
Lavender made itself into smoke
after the orange glow of a cigarette.

Lavender was the evening that interrupted the amber
reflection on the back of your neck.
Lavender soaked the words from the living
poet's mouth. It was lavender
that spoiled the tyranny of the Forsythia blooms.
It was lavender
that gave the air its melancholy.
Lavender is the stain on my sheets,
that remained after I tried
to bleach out the red. My sweat
made itself lavender in the fever
of the summer—it never got dark enough
long enough
to be any other way.

The dust that settled around her things
was not lavender
until she took her things with her.
Lavender is water when rinsing out a wine glass.
Lavender is blue trying to be yellow
in a creek. The creek has lavender
pebbles, smoothed by quiet legs made
of lavender.
Lavender was the smell that kept the rain
from being too heavy the morning I went
looking for him while he slept
alone somewhere on a street corner.
Lavender was the color of the entryway
to our house, and it became
more than lavender when we turned off the light and
went upstairs to bed.
The sound of the pipes at 4 a.m. was lavender,
and it made the house shudder.

My voice, when I whisper
about a gruesome fable, is lavender.
The color of your scalp is lavender, perforated
by follicles.

My umbilical cord was lavender.
Lavender sits gently on the center of the table,
but fills the whole room.
The hummingbird moths
felt most comfortable being around us,
and our chairs, when the moon shone
lavender on the magnolias.
The false stones on the side of the garage
were lavender. We projected
films all through
the summer night. Lavender
was the color of my father's
tears after we came back
to the green wallpaper of an empty house.

Lavender was the hole in the hand
of a stone saint
that I didn't dare touch to keep
my finger from being tinged lavender by blood.
Lavender was the thief of my mother's brother.
It settled
into him and wouldn't leave,
and then stole my father's brother.

Lavender was made by the sun
when it was being garish,
making everything brittle,
but faint. The room I was first alone in was lavender,
and its unmanageable glass doorknob
was lavender. Lavender was the scent of my mother
in the morning
when she sang loudly
to be certain I would wake up.
Lavender was when the spring came, and
the trees would become betwixt.
Your fists that pounded against
the cold ground began to turn
lavender
as you wept,
and people watched
from a balcony
across the street.

Revolutions Around a Madwoman

She frequently touches
new things
that were made to
look old; namely,
a silver necklace rusting
on the shelf in the bathroom.

She kisses—between
the eyebrows—
a child-woman/woman-child
sitting on the sink with bleeding toes.

Recall the old gestures
keep a lock of hair
keep many locks of hair
        weave them into a wreath for the mantle
arrange the furniture
over and over
sit on
again and again
    arrange the furniture
over and over

As we break in the new gestures
        put a glass case around a wreath
        place a velvet rope before a room, in the doorway
        make a convincing observation

The creek bed has pubic hair.
We were born there.

She looks up,
he looks to the other side.

When we left you had dirt
in the cut on the ball
of your foot.

You went to bed, after
rain mixed itself with the wine
in our glasses, and I became certain that it
was burning
holy water—
the stuff that touched the lips of every madwoman
you sent to the attic—that raw room
with one light bulb
and floorboards unashamed
of their in-between.

Those women were barefoot
and kept their mouths

to the same roundness

as a cat's pupils
in the dead of night.

The closest thing
to being back in the womb
is one's clean body
pressed tightly between
freshly washed
sheets.

Much like a gnat
flattened
near the spine of a
book—who can now be read with the text
as a new heavenly body, with the
same attitude
as tea leaves
in the transition of an
afternoon conversation.

After you fell asleep
in your cleanness,
the madwoman in the attic
heard your shoes
scraping beneath your bed
in revolutions around your body.

As moths, we tested our bodies
against the heated tubes
of the neon beer sign in the
corner of the bar
above the juke box
that two large
bald men—holding hands—
were standing next to.
The men were shouting:
One about kumquats and broken glass,
the other about bathroom stalls.
I smiled at them as we scorched
our skin in the same place

over and over,
and they stopped
shouting.

They whispered to me that it would be morning soon.

She watched you
hide cigarette butts
in the flowerbed and
eat the potato skins
she had left
for compost.
The madwoman set fire
to the garden and invited it
to remember itself
later next year.

The birds saw me sit there—
at the café table
when it had just become light
outside, before
she had a chance to arrive.
They were demanding breadcrumbs.
Breadcrumbs from the heels
of her loaves,
which I would never keep.

Their small heads were quick
and erect,
oscillating—the way
that the skittish
child-woman keeps her head
on the bus to avoid
glances from eyes and objects.

The madwoman found me,

and shooed me
from the birds
so that they would not get
the wrong impression.

Gathering Seeds

An old woman places
boots on the tips of thin
poles in the garden.
Their openings face downward
to the dirt.

The church on the street corner
marks the end
of the world.
The street it is on
doesn't continue past the limit
of one's own vision.
As we pick off ailments
from one another's skin—
those pink
scallops clinging
just below our ears—we
speak of brown,
aged plastic.

*The covering of a horse on springs
has turned suede
by increments of thighs in time.*
You said to me,
as you rolled the skin you removed
from above the corner
of my cheek
between your fingers.

A man returns home
from a three year trip
to the grocery store,
and finds an armchair—sleek,
with the mentality of a muse—
blocking and facing
the front entrance to his house.

He moves slowly around it, and
holds himself up in the doorway.
After keeping her head in the closet
for some indeterminable amount
of time, a woman stands up.
She tries to leave the house, but
stumbles into being a chair.

Strands of her hair fall between her legs.
They became small objects that clung
to the feet of strangers.
This pleased her.
In the front yard,
an old man has recovered a young man
while trying to bury scissors eight inches below the soil.

He sets off fireworks as warning
shots noting the arrival
of a young man.

His wife picks at her scabs, and recovers
feathered skin beneath them in response.

An Acquaintance

We saw the outline of a bull
in the twilight, and it saw our faces.

We saw its features,
filled its profile with cow eyes.
In the window sill
a framed pastoral scene
bobs in an aquarium.
The imaginary people
in the cottage's windows
could stare
at the place slightly
above a person's neck.
You used to be capable
of saving a horse
from human teeth.
Although we were hungry,
you'd let it drown
if sailing in certain latitudes.

One should only marry
the beasts of myths—those
holographic-eyed ones
that stall standing a hair's width
from the red siding of your house,
and can only be sighted
if their name has been spoken.
A marriage of this sort
makes a monkey of a man,
and a catfish of a girl.

After that, there is no change.
A red house becomes haunted when
slowly painted grey.
It has one light on, watching the other.

As We View *A Union of Sacred Monsters*

We think it might be easier
to collect small tins with
thinly painted prayers on one side.

Although they did little for the dying woman
who rests her head on a pillow—
with embroidery shaped in a language
you do not understand,

Wake up,
Heart,
Sleep.

It might be nice
to line the corners of the bedroom
with something we didn't make.

We have filled our pores
from the inside.

If these cells do not die
soon, we will be too large
for one another.
When I dream of the moment you
no longer speak to me,
you are a dead hummingbird
in my hand.

If I told you of this, you would
have us perform a superstitious exercise.
We would shift a circumference of candles around us
in and out to see
how far we can keep the ghosts from us
and still hear their voices.
We forbid each other
from saying words
like *machinery,*
because they remind us that
our teeth may rot
and that could be the only way
they can identify us
many years from now.

In the Time After

You wanted to observe every bird
in North America,
but did not want to know
any name that they had already been given.

When we saw a moth, you called it a bird.

I once had the shape
of a bird's body too, and a rapidly
paced circulatory system, but the things
that should have been feathers
are the color of ashes, and they are
the callouses on my feet.

Ceramics on the Face

How'd we get it to stick?
Oh, I know, you know.
We licked it first.

We are mirrors of each other only if
we paint our shadows
at opposite times of the day.

We made sure to be as ambiguous as possible
when we drink vodka
to make our lips drag.

If we keep it dermal,
with umbrella terms—we associate exercise
with stress stimulants and accidents.

Something happens
if the redness from not sweating
would have lived more presently.

When I left the house,
I never would have thought that
the word ugly would always be attached
to someone.
Wigs?
What is your wig?
A smile split evenly across
the face.

What Needs to Be an Essay

The problems
with painting and poetry are jumping
around, everywhere.
That is an interesting figure,
but not well-defined.
What is that weird thing in the foreground?
The clouds of this evening are moving
as a perfume puff of the female antagonist
who has a mystical appearance,
but has diamonds
in the eyes and heart.

I've forgotten to keep lists.
And so I have nothing to do.
My eyes are dry
this morning, because
we left three parties too early
and one too late
on Halloween.

The same images over and over.
I make limbs reach out from different joints,
but it's not all that different.
The sex.
I put varying features on the same
smells.

How can you talk
about quiet atrocities over a martini?
The skin all tastes the same too.
You want me to speak succinctly about trauma,
without being too disjointed.
And you want me to be funny too.
It seems like I'm witty. I smile all the time,
and make people laugh, you tell me.
The computer is trying to read me a poem
that is to be read flatly, it succeeds,
and it is flat.
Nothing is in order,
as you ask it to be.

Names

I've been mispronouncing my name for two decades.
This means I have been fooled at least twice.
Which rings faintly like the automated Christmas
music coming
somewhere from the tangled lights across the street
in January
or the invisible moment we decided to call them
cob webs
rather than spider webs.
How long did they get to belong to the spider?
We must've called it a cob web after it seemed to be pilling
like my baby quilt on the bed
that is too large for it.

I've done nothing, and there is dirt beneath my fingernails.
I wonder what my hands think they have been scraping.

Have I finally gotten the largest piece of the wallpaper
from the room that I've never set foot in?
I have only thought of that room
in the seconds where I see where I've come from.
Until now I've only gotten the tiny strips.

Sharp Pressure

There is a time when you know
that you missed your own private ceremony
for the last time the sandbox would be cleaned
out in the spring.
When the dead crickets
would stay there—sprinkled throughout,
not casually swept underneath the sand or to the corners.

Maybe the last goodbye to the sandbox
would have been last Easter
(if you're gonna be Christian, watch the Passion)
when you knowingly check for the chocolate eggs
covered in pastel foil will be neatly placed on top of the grit
by your mother, and your reward for creaking the cover open
was conspicuously sitting there.
That would have been a great last time.

You had your first pimple popped
by someone else.

In front of the mirror that you know your father took
from his mother's house
(the one that bred horses) seems ancient.
Its edges are flooding with
frozen black water.
Tiny little pools of dark that hover near your face
as you watch your father gather a small bit of skin
and you wait
for brief, sharp pressure.
Every time there are loud noises, focus on your skin.

You might also remember those layers of yellow
that came with the humidity in the summer,
would stick to the white paint in the upstairs bathroom,
and continually gather dust through the winter.
The green shag carpet hid everything else.
No evidence of the water
sneaking out of the shower in the morning
when you were still blind. You were the first one awake
by your neon orange dollar store alarm clock,
the house was still full of the night.

You tried to make breakfast
(you were a premature mother hen
and only could make toast with brown sugar).
You stood in the hallway naked with your sisters
when one of them tried to fling her wet
towel over the shower rod
after bath-time and it hit the low-hanging glass
covering of the light bulb,
you shivered together in the dark hallway
underneath your baby portraits.
The green carpet didn't go that far—the wood floor
chilled you all the way up to the back of your necks
as your father loudly admonished you all and
carefully picked up all the small shards
from between the fibers.

You might remember the time you touched yourself
(the first time)
 years later, lying on top of that green carpet.
You didn't know how, really.

Didn't learn about the more
sensitive spots in sex-ed, but
you knew there was something there.
You felt dirty like the carpet,
but you didn't feel right in your bed.
You recall having told someone you didn't know how.

The largest difference between then and now is at the time,
you could not feel the persistent labor
of muscles beneath your eyes, which made them
easier to keep wide most of the time.

When you woke up on the day you and he went to go get cheap Mexican food,
before you decided to go, you were still sweaty.
It was two in the afternoon in September.
It is so nice to hang out without guilt.
He was accustomed to your sense of humor,
and you knew that should have been funny.
The sun came in
dirty through the streaked windshield.

It was difficult to get your feet on the ground
of the car with all
the trash from gas station food mixed
with books and various print-outs.

As you drove, he sat next to you and talked.
You only heard parts of him
through your own mumbling of apologies
softly so that the bagpipes would cover them up.
You were hoping that among the rubble, the books would be most visible,
not the fried food residue—but you hoped that the titles were not legible,
so that no one could ask any questions.

He was musing about the beauty and honesty of insects, to be odd.
He was repeating himself.
You remember that only male crickets chirp.

And then you remember that track you listened to of a cricket's song
slowed down to the speed of a human's heart beat,
how it sounded symphonic.

All Legs

I leaned over and saw
One thousand baby spiders in tow
on the back
of a large momma spider.

What does a mother do in the face
of a camera
with so many eyes?

When I decide to perform myself
I am a bird
unwittingly
picking up shards of glass
with my beak.

I taste light refracting.
I taste the history of photography—women posed
passing through light and
quotation marks.

Materials for Birth

We still behave as though we were born by breaking
loose from the head of a Titan.

If something is burning, we are responsible
for telling someone, or suffocating it, so
we are careful
to only look at the whites of each other's eyes.

You speak with the urgency of a child
misplaced in the super market, but never raise
your voice any louder than an infant's
breath while sleeping.

It is not our interiors
that make us
become our mothers and fathers,
it is the moment we know that they will die, and
they have begun to.

We become them
by starting with their extremities—
a hand creased by habit, and legs traced with blue.
The sounds of their largeness come next,
and this is only remembered from the time we first learned
to crane our necks upward.
We find that white is only a color when it is dirty.

In our central room, we keep a glass shelf
stocked with painted porcelain—small and pastel
boys and lambs. The girls are unpainted,
except for their lips, which are faintly pink.

Every time I see a glass shelf, there must be porcelain.
As my eyes place porcelain on the glass, I think
It's starting to look like an actual place.

If ever we should fall asleep under a tree in the cemetery,
it will be near a family plot.
We will wake up and make love.
Berries will fall from the trees and we will move with them.
Our skin will become road work orange
after they burst beneath us,
but will turn to the tone of nearly dried blood.

Outside, the Inside

She knows the importance of a name.
She changed hers
(I don't think legally).
She likes that it means *generous*
in a culture that is dead
except for its linguistic contributions
to modern day Iran.
For another culture, it meant *spring*.
She likes the ambiguity of that.

We mostly talk about absurdity.
We feel similarly about a lot of things
dealing with sexual encounters.
She's blunt about it, which is a relief to me.
One time she looked at me squarely
You know we are both plain-looking.
But we have a large
presence in the room.
Something they can't name.

I looked away from her eyes
and settled on her chest.
It is covered
with very real
skin stars.
They still make me think of the fake stars
in an indoor roller-coaster.
I can't ever remember what it's called.

The roller-coaster is dark
enough so that you can only vaguely see
the outline of the architecture
underneath the small stars, but the stars
are just bright
enough that they are
what makes you remember
you are inside.

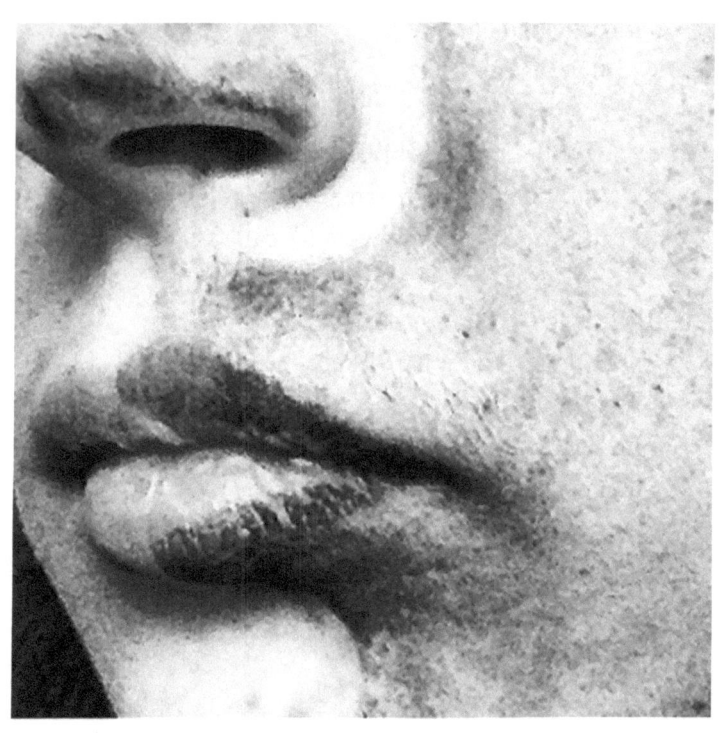

www.ingramcontent.com/pod-product-compliance
Lightning Source LLC
Chambersburg PA
CBHW030138100526
44592CB00011B/948